BUREAU OF LAND MANAGEMENT–
Montana/Dakotas

National Landscape Conservation System

NLCS Strategy:
2013–2016

NATIONAL CONSERVATION LANDS

BLM

Montana/Dakotas

Upper Missouri River Breaks National Monument

Dear Friends of the Montana/Dakotas BLM,

I am pleased to share our strategic approach to managing the Montana/Dakotas National Conservation Lands as part of the National Landscape Conservation System. These lands represent some of the most scenic, culturally rich, and scientifically important of all public lands managed by the Bureau of Land Management in our three-state region.

The BLM manages Pompeys Pillar and Upper Missouri River Breaks national monuments; the 149-mile Upper Missouri Wild and Scenic River; the Beartrap Canyon Wilderness Area (the first to be established in the nation); 39 wilderness study areas; the Lewis and Clark and Nez Perce national historic trails; and a segment of the Continental Divide Trail. It is an honor to have such an important responsibility entrusted to us by the American people and we do not take this role lightly.

The Washington Office developed a national strategy in 2011 to clearly lay out the principles by which the BLM will manage National Conservation Lands units. The strategy was developed on the heels of the NLCS Summit, commemorating the 10-year anniversary of the National Landscape Conservation System, where BLM gathered input from our various partners and cooperators.

This strategy does not replace the resource management plans developed in collaboration with other agencies and the public, but it does lay out the process by which my staff will evaluate our status and prioritize our efforts in achieving stated goals for these conservation units. In doing so, we sought input from our partners and stakeholders through the assistance of our Resource Advisory Councils. Considering your input, I am fully committed to advancing this four-year strategy in the Montana/Dakotas and look forward to its implementation.

We are committed to responsibly managing these lands in partnership with the numerous stakeholders that depend on the land, whether for recreation, drinking water, scientific research or to support their livelihoods. Implementation of this strategy would not be feasible without your contributions. Together we will ensure that National Conservation Lands will benefit the people of Montana/Dakotas and all Americans.

Sincerely,

Jamie E. Connell

Jamie E. Connell
BLM Montana/Dakotas State Director

BLM Montana/Dakotas National Landscape Conservation System

Your Land. Your Treasure.

Introduction

The Montana/Dakotas National Landscape Conservation System (NLCS) Strategy will implement the BLM's National Landscape Conservation System 15-Year Strategy 2010-2025 for designated public lands in Montana and the Dakotas over the next four years. It will also provide a starting point for discussion with partners, stakeholders, and members of the public on how they can support the management of these special places.

Some actions in this strategy are intended to implement the bureau-wide actions identified in the 15-year national strategy, and others are Montana/Dakotas-specific based on the national framework. This document is intended to guide the thought processes and inform the management and budget decisions that Montana/Dakotas will make to ensure stewardship of the National Landscape Conservation System units in our states.

It is important to understand the purpose, context, and limitations of this strategy. Implementation is contingent on budget and staffing, consistency with law, policy and approved decisions, and the level of support from our partners and cooperators. The strategy itself does not amend BLM land use plans or replace local-level planning or decision-making processes. It is a "living" document that will be regularly updated as successes are achieved, priorities updated, and opportunities arise.

Some of the actions it contains will be accomplished by the State Office, and some are state-wide actions that will be implemented by respective district or field offices and their partners and volunteers. It describes the approach that BLM-Montana/Dakotas will pursue over the next four years to implement the National Landscape Conservation System Strategy, but it does not conceive of doing it all. That is, only a few of these actions will begin in 2013, with other beginning as late as 2016. Also, some of the actions described do not apply to every office, conservation designation type, or acre of public land. This allows for local interpretation of state- and national-level strategic goals and priorities. This strategy also provides the foundation for the development of site-specific management actions.

This strategy will help inform readers of the direction that BLM-Montana/Dakotas will take to achieve its mission to conserve, protect, and restore the nationally significant lands in Montana/Dakotas that were designated for their outstanding values. We invite you to see yourself or your organization in the actions that follow, and to work with us to achieve our common goals.

For additional information on this strategy, contact BLM-Montana/Dakotas National Landscape Conservation System Lead, Dave Lefevre, at (406) 896-5037 or at dlefevre@blm.gov.

Humbug Spires Wilderness Study Area

What is the National Landscape Conservation System?

The National Landscape Conservation System is a collection of special areas administered by the Bureau of Land Management that were designated by the president or Congress for conservation, protection, and restoration of their outstanding resources and values, for the benefit of current and future generations. Nationally, there are more than 880 areas, including national monuments, national conservation areas, national scenic and historic trails, wild and scenic rivers, wilderness areas, wilderness study areas and other congressionally and presidentially designated lands. These areas are characteristic of the diversity of the West itself – from coastal trails to arctic tundra, from mountain peaks to desert dunes.

The System was created by Secretarial Order in 2000 under President Bill Clinton. It was codified on March 30, 2009, when President Barack Obama signed the Omnibus Public Land Management Act: "In order to conserve, protect, and restore nationally significant landscape that have outstanding cultural, ecological, and scientific values for the benefit of current and future generations, there is established in the Bureau of Land Management the National Landscape Conservation System." The law directs the Secretary of the Interior to "manage the system in accordance with any applicable law (including regulations) relating to any component of the system... and in a manner that protects the values for which the components of the system were designated."

National Landscape Conservation System lands in Montana/Dakotas

The BLM-Montana/Dakotas manages 46 conservation units, covering nearly a million acres of public lands that BLM administers. From the high desert badlands in southeastern Montana to the alpine peaks along the Continental Divide in southwestern Montana, the conservation lands represent a cross-section of the state's most pristine, iconic, and treasured places. Montana/Dakotas manages the first BLM wilderness area (Beartrap Canyon Wilderness) and large sections of the river corridors traveled by Lewis and Clark during their epic expedition.

The uses of these lands are many – livestock grazing, energy development, minerals, forest products, rights-of-way, Native American traditional uses, recreation, wildlife habitat, and conservation. With that diversity of needs and uses comes a tall order: The BLM is responsible for balancing this formidable mix of practices to sustain the health, diversity, and productivity of public land for present and future generations. All the pieces add up to a dynamic, challenging and rewarding system of public land management.

The NLCS represents a model in which landscape-scale conservation can be achieved through shared stewardship. To carry out its NLCS mission, the BLM seeks the help of tribes, communities, private landowners, Friends groups, recreationists, ranchers, business interests, universities, and others to assist in managing for conservation in the context of a larger working landscape and to respect the unique and diverse opportunities that result from these national treasures.

Conserving and managing these significant landscapes is a tremendous responsibility, and BLM-Montana/Dakotas is privileged to work with the numerous partners, friends groups, and volunteers to achieve these important goals.

Centennial Wilderness Study Area

Conservation Designations in Montana
- **National Monuments:** Upper Missouri River Breaks, Pompeys Pillar
- **Wild and Scenic Rivers:** Upper Missouri River
- **National Historic and Scenic Trails:** Lewis and Clark, Nez Perce, Continental Divide
- **Wilderness:** Beartrap Canyon Wilderness Area
- **Wilderness Study Areas:** 39 units statewide

Implementing State Director Priorities

Axolotl Lakes Wilderness Study Area

Many of the actions included in this strategy address specific objectives of the BLM State Director's priorities. For example:

Embrace Landscape Conservation to Sustain and Restore Healthy Lands, Communities and Wildlife Populations:

- Completing Rapid Ecoregional and Ethnographic Assessments for National Landscape Conservation System (NLCS) units and adjacent lands.

- Working with partner agencies, stakeholders, and tribes to identify focal areas for resource conservation and restoration efforts in NLCS units.

- Participating in Joint Ventures, Landscape Conservation Cooperatives, and Climate Science Centers.

- Showcase America's Great Outdoors (AGO) projects and implement the National Landscape Conservation System (NLCS) strategy to collaboratively manage NLCS units as part of the larger landscape and raise awareness of the values and benefits of landscape conservation.

Enhance public enjoyment of BLM lands through diverse recreation opportunities, high-quality information, and improved access and consolidated management:

- Define and communicate the BLM recreation niche in Montana and the Dakotas.

- Work with the access board of directors and the land tenure specialists to identify and prioritize key access opportunities with emphasis on providing access to large blocks of public land within NLCS units. Prioritize conservation acquisitions in National Monuments, WSAs and National Trail Corridors.

- Coordinate travel management planning with U.S. Forest Service, U.S. Fish and Wildlife Service, National Park Service, and state agencies to provide consistent route designations where routes cross multiple jurisdictions.

- Expand and improve the Montana/Dakotas communication products, including the Access and Recreation web pages.

- Establish or continue partnerships with local law enforcement, including through reimbursable agreements, to provide highly visible patrols within the NLCS units and to assist BLM law enforcement rangers.

Showcase BLM Montana/Dakotas to build trust and credibility, enhance public service and enjoyment, and engage citizens in stewardship and decision making

- Develop and implement an external communications plan for Montana/Dakotas NLCS.

- Update Recreation.gov for all destination sites to identify recreation opportunities available within and near conservation units.

- Develop and conduct field trips to involve the public, key decision makers, and the media about the importance of managing Montana/Dakotas NLCS areas, and inspire individuals to participate constructively in increasing support for these areas.

- Broaden America's Great Outdoors (AGO) partnerships on the Upper Missouri River and in other settings where interest and opportunities emerge.

Uphold sound fiscal health to be as efficient as possible and responsibly use the public's money :

- Identify Service First opportunities and develop an interagency collaboration strategy.

- Work with partners to pursue external funding opportunities and resources such as grants, volunteers and in-kind contributions to implement mutually beneficial activities.

Build Native American relations and partnerships that result in mutual trust and respect, establish lasting government-to-government relationships, fully implement our trust responsibilities, and diversify our workforce:

- Implement mutually beneficial projects such as native plants programs and ethnographic landscape assessments.

- Coordinate and initiate formal agreements for traditional cultural use studies in NLCS units.

- Use and expand agreements with tribal colleges to engage Native American youth and build tribal relationships in NLCS units.

Engage youth in current and future public lands stewardship:

- Employing and mentoring youth, who are the future stewards of the National System of Public Lands.

- Providing interpretation and environmental education programs as a way to raise awareness of public land resources and encourage stewardships.

- Leveraging resources by seeking opportunities such as Montana Conservation Corps and partnerships with universities.

- Developing assistance agreements to further promote youth partnerships for employment and project implementation.

BLM Montana/Dakotas National

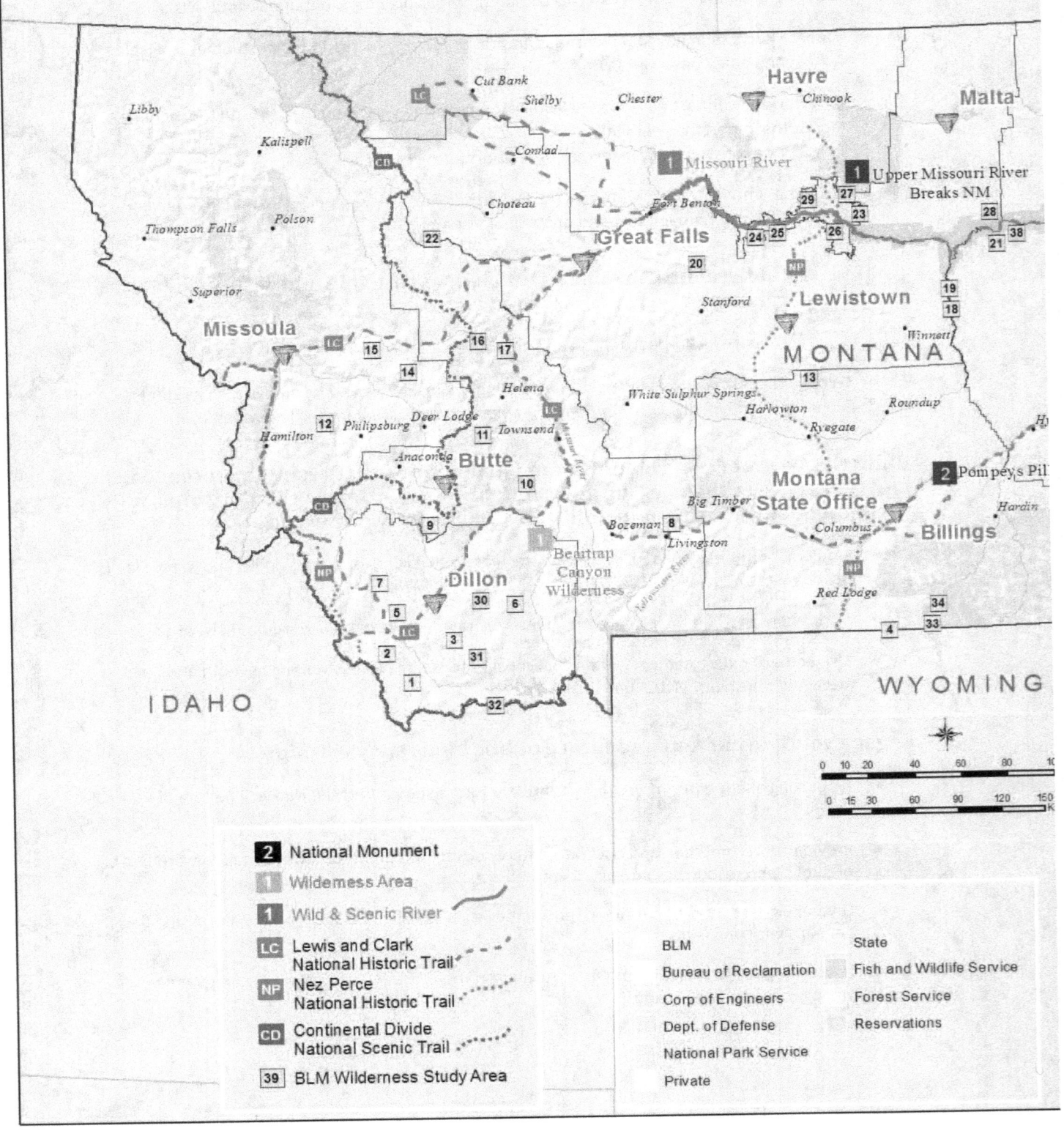

Libby •   Cut Bank   Shelby •   Chester •   **Havre**   Chinook •   **Malta**

Kalispell •   Conrad •   Missouri River   Upper Missouri River Breaks NM

Thompson Falls •   Polson •   Choteau •   Fort Benton   **Great Falls**

Superior •   22   20   Stanford •   **Lewistown**   Winnett •

Missoula   15   16   17   **MONTANA**

14   Helena •   White Sulphur Springs •   13   Harlowton •   Roundup •

12   Philipsburg •   Deer Lodge •   Townsend •   Ryegate •

11   Anaconda •   **Butte**   10   **Montana State Office**   Pompeys Pil

9   Big Timber •   Columbus •   Hardin

Beartrap Canyon Wilderness   Bozeman •   8   Livingston •   **Billings**

7   **Dillon**   30   6   Red Lodge •

5   34   33

2   3   31   4

1   **IDAHO**   32   **WYOMING**

27   29   23   24   25   26   28   38   21   19   18

Scale: 0 10 20 40 60 80 100

0 15 30 60 90 120 150 K

Legend

- **2** National Monument
- **1** Wilderness Area
- **1** Wild & Scenic River
- **LC** Lewis and Clark National Historic Trail
- **NP** Nez Perce National Historic Trail
- **CD** Continental Divide National Scenic Trail
- **39** BLM Wilderness Study Area

BLM — State
Bureau of Reclamation — Fish and Wildlife Service
Corp of Engineers — Forest Service
Dept. of Defense — Reservations
National Park Service
Private

Landscape Conservation System

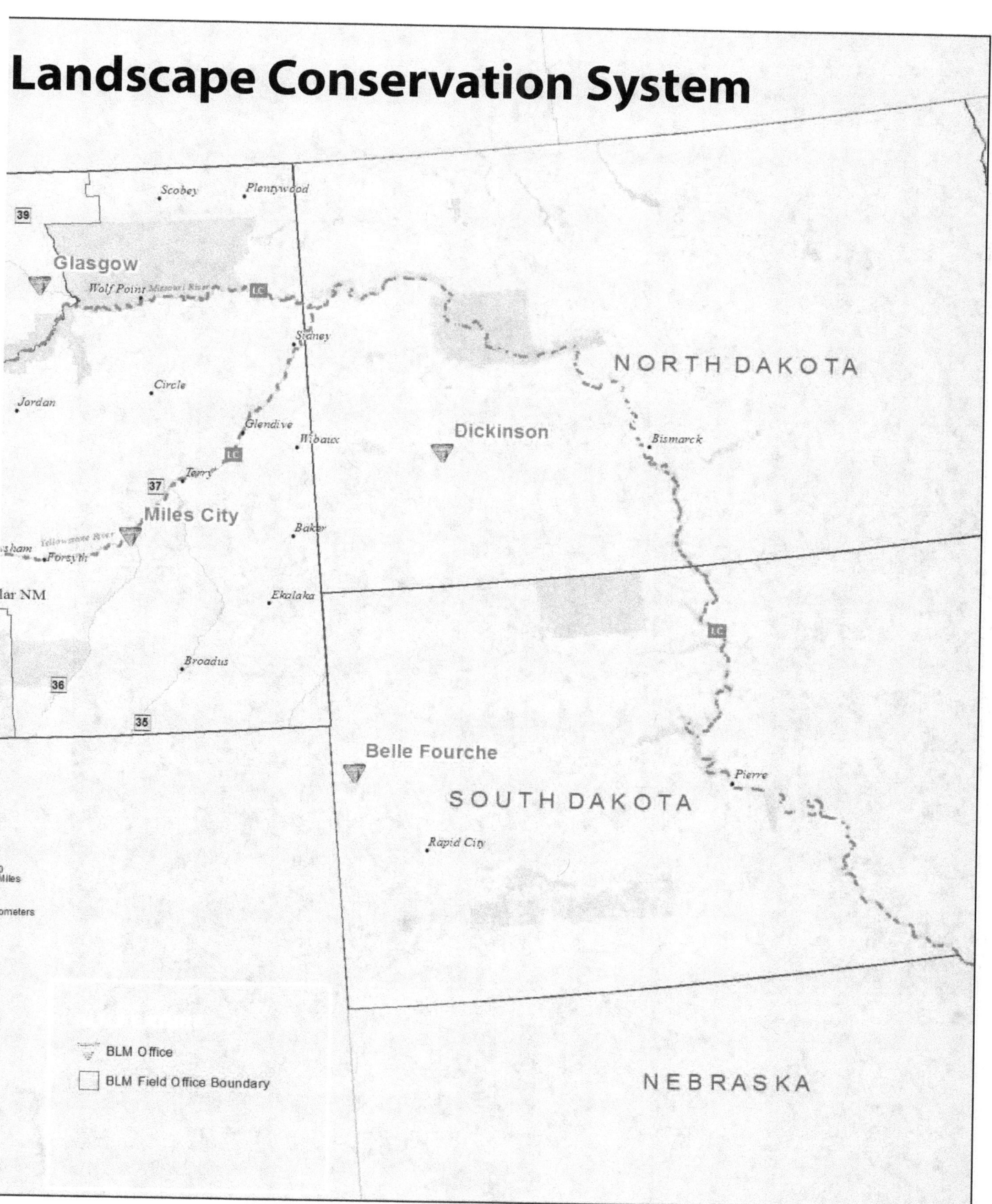

Terry Badlands Wilderness Study Area

NATIONAL LANDSCAPE CONSERVATION SYSTEM STRATEGY

The National Landscape Conservation System Strategy (NLCS) for Montana/Dakotas outlined below is structured under the four main themes and priority goals developed for the national strategy. Under each theme, BLM-Montana/Dakotas has included a short statement identifying the state's strategic approach. To implement each goal, BLM-Montana/Dakotas has identified a number of action items that will be a focus over the next four years. Additional detailed tasks and implementing actions are not included within the document and will be developed during implementation.

Theme 1: Ensuring the Conservation, Protection, and Restoration of NLCS Values. Primacy of conservation within the NLCS lands, how science serves to further conservation, and to provide for compatible use that protects NLCS resources and values.

Theme 2: Collaboratively Managing the NLCS Lands as Part of the Larger Landscape. Building a better conservation model through collaborative management.

Theme 3: Raising Awareness of the Value and Benefits of the BLM's NLCS Lands. Raise public awareness and understanding of the NLCS lands, cultivate relationships, promote community stewardship of BLM-managed public land, and provide for use and enjoyment of present and future generations.

Theme 4: Building upon BLM's Commitment to Conservation. Promote a model of conservation excellence internally, through improved understanding and fully integrating the NLCS within the BLM.

Upper Missouri River Breaks National Monument

Theme 1: Ensuring the Conservation, Protection, and Restoration of NLCS Values

Strategic Approach: Capitalize on the present opportunity to incorporate direction from the national strategy and identify new policy direction through the multiple, on-going resource management plan (RMP) revisions. The RMPs will do the following to ensure conservation:

- *Place emphasis on resources at risk, such as threatened and endangered species, heritage resources and other resources unique to Montana/Dakotas, and the other nationally significant resources that were specified in the proclamation or enabling legislation.*

- *Provide detailed guidance and a framework for project level planning and environmental review.*

Improve the understanding and documentation of NLCS resource values, their condition, and potential threats by emphasizing the completion of baseline inventories, bolstering research and science programs, sharing and integrating information with other resource managers (outside BLM), and through the development of comprehensive monitoring programs for NLCS objects and values.

Goal 1A: Clearly communicate that the conservation, protection, and restoration of NLCS values is the highest priority in NLCS planning and management, consistent with the designating legislation or presidential proclamation.

1. Conduct trainings to assist district and field offices with implementation of the new NLCS manuals.

2. Develop and implement standard process for documenting monument objects and conservation values for NLCS units on which to base environmental analysis.

3. Measure existing conditions, identify desired conditions, and document impacts from management actions or programs.

4. Review and update activity level plans that impact conservation lands.

Conservation Lands Foundation

The Conservation Lands Foundation (CLF) is the only non-governmental organization dedicated solely to partnering with BLM friends group organizations. We work in partnership with CLF and its network to conserve, protect and restore the National Landscape Conservation System (NLCS) lands in Montana. The CLF's mission is to collaborate and assist BLM-Montana/Dakotas through education, public involvement and development of friends groups and other partnerships to support the conservation system. The foundation has developed and implemented a successful grant program that provides funds and other resources to friends groups and other organizations that support conservation efforts for Montana's NLCS lands. As one of the four original member organizations, Friends of the Missouri River Breaks has received more than $300,000 since 2008 to support organizational development, training for board and staff development, restoration activities and other conservation projects, and media and communications training. A new partnership with the Pompeys Pillar Historical Association for 2013 is expected to strengthen their capacity to provide education and other public services for the monument.

Beartrap Canyon Wilderness Area

- Update or revise the Upper Missouri National Wild and Scenic River Management Plan

- Update or revise the Beartrap Canyon Wilderness Management Plan

- Review and revise allotment and coordinated management plans as needed.

5. Ensure that adequate documentation for conservation units is developed and maintained.

   - Develop and maintain serialized case files for each NLCS unit and include legislation, maps, complete boundary descriptions and surveys.

   - Update master title plats to identify national trails corridors.

   - Document annual plan maintenance actions as appropriate.

6. Ensure that new, revised and amended RMPs identify goals, objectives, and management actions to protect conservation values.

   - Develop guidance and templates to supplement the planning handbook that incorporate adequate documentation of NLCS values/objects and meets NEPA and public involvement criteria.

   - Conduct plan conformance reviews of existing RMPs to gauge effectiveness in protecting conservation values. Identify the need for plan amendments or maintenance actions to ensure conformance with updated policy manuals.

7. Work with ranchers and other landowners to attain conservation of rangelands at a watershed or landscape scale. Develop collaborative management solutions to ensure that range conditions are achieving standards or trending positively. Implement livestock grazing guidelines when reviewing and reauthorizing grazing permits. Also, consider innovative measures to more effectively manage livestock to address resource conditions, including for restoration purposes.

Goal 1B: Expand understanding of the NLCS values through assessment, inventory, and monitoring.

1. Identify high risk, un-surveyed boundaries and prioritize cadastral needs.

2. Develop a Management of Land Boundaries Plan for units that have a high potential for oil and gas or mineral development, such as the Upper Missouri River Breaks National Monument.

3. Develop and implement a standardized wilderness/WSA monitoring program.

Theme 1: Ensuring Conservation of NLCS Values

- Establish GPS data dictionaries and geodatabases to capture and store consistent electronic field data.

- Create user-friendly monitoring program for use by partners and volunteers.

4. Monitor the physical condition, amount and type of use taking place on "ways" that are open to motorized use. Take appropriate measures to return the way(s) to pre-designation conditions.

5. Develop statistically-based predictive models for cultural resources in areas of low, moderate, and high resource potential to better manage NLCS units and adjacent areas.

6. Assess and document the paleontological potential of all NLCS units through the use of on-the-ground pedestrian examination of fossil producing geologic formations.

7. Conduct integrated land health assessments at a watershed or planning unit level using established protocols. Monitor and evaluate vegetation to ensure sustainable habitats and forage supplies.

Goal 1C: Provide a scientific foundation for decision-making.

1. Develop a science strategy to engage the scientific community that highlights opportunities for research or synthesis of existing scientific data. The strategy would include:

- Appointing a lead to facilitate statewide coordination and identify champions for planning and implementation of the science program within NLCS units.

- Developing outreach products to engage the scientific community, including universities.

- Developing partnerships with universities, federal science agencies and professional societies through existing agreements such as cooperative ecosystem study units, landscape conservation cooperatives, and climate change centers .

- In consortium with partners, developing and hosting a science symposium at one of the monuments or field offices in proximity to conservation lands.

Friends of the Missouri Breaks Monument

As the only local advocacy group working to protect the Upper Missouri River Breaks National Monument, the Friends help BLM achieve its mission for management of the Monument by educating the public, advocating for responsible access and environmentally responsible uses, and supporting groups and agencies that protect and restore the Monument. The Friends have been actively involved in National Public Lands Day events, other recreation site maintenance projects and volunteer resource monitoring.

2012 Volunteers

During the 2012 fiscal year, BLM-Montana/ Dakotas volunteers contributed more than 6,000 hours of work toward NLCS lands.

Pompeys Pillar National Monument

Goal 1D: Use the NLCS as an outdoor laboratory and demonstration center for new and innovative management that aid in the conservation, protection, and restoration of NLCS areas.

1. Develop "citizen science" partnerships with interested and affiliated groups to share assessment, inventory, and monitoring tasks that support priority management needs and existing plans.

2. Provide training opportunities for Montana Conservation Corps (MCC) to develop crew skills (i.e. saw training, wilderness monitoring, sage grouse fence marking, and restoration practices (weed treatment/route decommissioning).

3. Explore opportunities to develop reserve allotments to help reduce livestock impacts in critical watersheds during times when adequate forage is not available.

Goal 1E: Limit discretionary uses to those compatible with the conservation, protection, and restoration of the values for which NLCS lands were designated.

1. Identify and catalog valid existing rights and grandfathered uses to clarify discretionary decision space. Do not authorize discretionary uses that cannot be managed in a manner compatible with desigating authorities.

2. Complete travel management planning for NLCS units to ensure adequate access without compromising the conservation values and purposes for the designation.

3. Evaluate the necessity and potential impacts from Special Recreation Permit proposals to ensure that conservation values are a key consideration prior to renewing or authorizing any new permits or activities.

4. Develop supplemental regulations for WSAs to provide enforcement capability and to prevent the establishment of new discretionary uses, such as mountain biking, the use of game carts or motorized equipment, that may preclude potential designation.

5. As appropriate, incorporate these actions into current plan revisions or amendments.

Goal 1F: Manage facilities in a manner that conserves, protects, and restores NLCS values.

1. Complete inventories and eligibility determinations for all structures within conservation units. Remove or allow to deteriorate those structures that are not significant historic properties or necessary to provide safety or resource protections, or administration of valid uses.

2. Implement an active route rehabilitation program in WSAs and other conservation lands with route designations. Allocate funding to support youth conservation corps projects.

3. Inventory entrance and boundary signage to identify additional needs. Develop and implement sign plans to ensure public knowledge of appropriate uses and area regulations.

4. Support the development and shared management of heritage education facilities and visitor services in gateway communities. Examples include the partnerships with the City of Fort Benton and the River and Plains Society to manage the Upper Missouri River Breaks Interpretive Center.

5. Maintain a sustainable transportation network including non-motorized trails. Consider trail development or modifications that enhance visitor experiences and protect the area's natural and cultural resource values.

Montana Conservation Corps

For 20 years, the Montana Conservation Corps has partnered with the BLM to assist with resource management projects such as trail construction/maintenance, noxious weed eradication, range improvement maintenance and construction, forest restoration, and wildlife improvement projects. The MCC's mission is to inspire young people through hands-on conservation service to be leaders, stewards of the land and engaged citizens who improve their communities. The MCC provides a variety of conservation crews including expedition crews consisting of high school-aged members who serve six- week tours during the summer season, young adult crews who serve year-round tours, and veterans crews who receive training and certification in wildfire management. The MCC has been integral in meeting BLM's youth hiring targets over the past several years. In 2012 alone, over 170 youth were employed to implement BLM projects statewide, with over 17,000 hours of service.

Upper Missouri River Breaks National Monument

Theme 2: Collaboratively Managing NLCS lands as Part of the Larger Landscape

Strategic Approach: Identify a collaborative regional approach to developing projects by coordinating with regional partners to accomplish landscape-level inventory and monitoring, manage shared facilities, and utilize innovative practices that improve efficiency and effectiveness.

- *Identify and target partnership opportunities with other agencies, tribal and state governments, service communities, and private land and water managers. Focus on areas where linear NLCS resources (trails, rivers) cross jurisdictional boundaries and where conservation lands are adjacent to similarly managed lands.*

Goal 2A: Emphasize an ecosystem-based approach to manage the NLCS in the context of the surrounding landscape.

1. Use the Northern Rockies & Northern Great Plains Rapid Ecological Assessments (REAs) to identify areas in and around NLCS units that are important for resource protection and conservation within a broader landscape context; such as providing for large-scale wildlife corridors and water dependent resources.

2. Complete the ethnographic components of the REAs to identify and assess cultural significance of landscapes.

3. Continue to prioritize non-native, invasive plant assessments and weed eradication in partnership with counties, state and private landowners.

Goal 2B: Adopt a cross-jurisdictional, community-based approach to landscape-level conservation planning and management.

1. Implement the Missouri River America's Great Outdoors project in collaboration with local partners.

2. Participate in the Great Northern & Prairie Plains and Potholes Landscape Conservation Cooperative to enable and integrate conservation of NLCS units within the larger landscape context.

3. Continue to partner with the National Park Service and U.S. Forest Service trail administrators and preservation groups, and neighboring states to ensure consistent and effective cross-jurisdictional conservation planning and management of National Historic Trails.

4. Coordinate an annual conservation lands summit with agency partners including the U.S. Forest Service, National Park Service, U.S. Fish and Wildlife Service, Montana Fish, Wildlife and Parks, and Bureau of Reclamation. Work closely with partners and internal staff to share success stories and lessons learned.

5. Work with the access board of directors and the land tenure specialists to identify and prioritize key access opportunities with emphasis on providing access to large blocks of public land within NLCS units.

6. Support the Cottonwood Restoration Task Force in cooperation with the Bureau of Reclamation, Army Corps of Engineers and U.S. Fish and Wildlife Service.

7. Coordinate travel management planning with U.S. Forest Service, U.S. Fish and Wildlife Service, National Park Service, state and local agencies and private landowners to provide consistent route designations where routes cross multiple jurisdictions.

8. Continue cooperative efforts with Pennsylvania Power and Light of Montana (PPLM) and other partners to collectively manage the Lewis and Clark National Historic Trail. All recreation sites within the trail corridor will continue to be managed in a manner that promotes public accessibility, resource protection, visitor safety, and interpretive opportunities.

9. Where relevant and possible, such as for landscape species or continuity of a riparian system, work with adjacent public and private landowners on science and conservation to ensure an ecosystem approach.

Goal 2C: Work with Congress, tribes, other federal and state agencies, and national and local communities to identify and protect lands that are critical to the long-term ecological sustainability of the landscape.

1. Coordinate with Montana Department of Transportation and local governments to provide recreational signing, auto tours and wayside exhibits on public roads and information about visitor services in gateway communities.

2. Identify Service First opportunities and develop an interagency collaboration strategy to gain efficiencies in conducting common tasks such as WSA monitoring.

3. Develop a prioritized list of potential acquisitions or scenic conservation easements to protect objects of historical/cultural/recreational value. Pursue opportunities with willing sellers to develop strong Land and Water Conservation Fund proposals annually.

Pompeys Pillar Historical Association

Long-time supporters of conservation protection for Pompeys Pillar National Monument, the Association strives, to develop the historic potential of Pompeys Pillar National Monument, the site of the only remaining physical evidence on the trail of the Lewis and Clark Expedition of 1803-1806."

Each year, PPHA provides volunteers and staff to operate the bookstore/gift shop at the interpretive center, providing critical public information and educational resources. The PPHA is integral to the success of the annual Clark Days event, which attracts over 2,000 participants each summer to commemorate William Clark's stop at the site on July 25, 1806, during his trip down the Yellowstone River. In 2012, 37 PPHA volunteers provided over 4,000 hours to help BLM protect and enhance the nationally significant resource of the Monument.

Holter Lake - Sleeping Giant Wilderness Study Area

4. Work collaboratively with the State of Montana and lease holders to develop priorities for the exchange of state lands within the Upper Missouri River Breaks National Monument for other BLM lands outside of the monument.

5. Coordinate and initiate formal agreements for traditional cultural use studies in NLCS units.

6. Establish or continue partnerships with local law enforcement, including through reimbursable agreements, to provide highly visible patrols within the NLCS units and to assist BLM law enforcement rangers.

7. Develop a cooperative agreement with Montana Fish, Wildlife and Parks to support management and acquisition of public access within the Lewis and Clark National Historic Trail corridor.

Goal 2D: Adopt a community-based approach to recreation and visitor services delivery, consistent with the conservation purpose of the NLCS and the socio-economic goals of the local community.

1. Continue to participate in local tourism boards (Russell Country, Yellowstone Country, and Southeast Montana) to highlight opportunities on BLM NLCS lands.

2. Provide representation on the State of Montana Tourism Advisory Council and at the annual Governor's Council on Tourism Conference to showcase BLM resources.

3. Contribute to regional tourism efforts by providing information for exhibits, maps, and webpages that promote recreation opportunities in and near local communities. Explore geotourism opportunities with National Geographic and other local agency efforts.

4. Work with partners to pursue external funding opportunities and resources such as grants, volunteers and in-kind contributions to implement mutually beneficial activities.

5. Utilize a geotourism approach to highlight and preserve unique cultural and natural values of gateway communities. Explore opportunities to partner with National Geographic and other partners through existing nationwide agreements.

Beartrap Canyon Wilderness Area

Humbug Spires Wilderness Study Area

Theme 3: Raising Awareness of the Value and Benefits of the NLCS

Strategic Approach: Utilize outreach approaches that reach the largest numbers of visitors and users by emphasizing outreach to educational institutions, collaborating with national, regional and local tourism promoters, and through increased marketing at high visitation sites.

Goal 3A: Launch a long-term public awareness initiative about the BLM's NLCS lands, including national and local outreach, communications, and media plans.

1. Develop and implement an external communications plan for Montana/Dakotas with emphasis on:

   - Developing a consistent NLCS message for use in all media.

   - Developing maps and webpages for all NLCS units (update 100K maps with unit boundaries).

   - Ensuring that all marketing, advertising, notices, informational kiosks, websites and signs for conservation units highlight that they are part of the NLCS.

   - Expanding the use of all forms of media, especially non-traditional methods, such as social media, films, and other digital applications.

   - Explaining what the different units of the conservation system are, how are they designated/established, and the values they are intended to protect.

   - Developing partnerships with local and national magazines, television programs, and other tourism promoters.

   - Facilitating relationships between counties/local government and BLM.

   - Developing materials in languages other than English.

   - Implementing branding efforts, using our new tag line/slogan "Your Land. Your Treasure."

   - Creating a publication distribution network across conservation lands and high-use visitor sites.

   - Partner with local service organizations to support promotion and access to NLCS lands.

2. Update Recreation.gov for all destination sites to identify recreation opportunities available within and near conservation units.

3. Develop and conduct field trips to involve the public, key decision makers, and the media about the importance of managing Montana/Dakotas NLCS areas, and inspire individuals to participate constructively in increasing support for these areas.

4. Participate with interagency partners to celebrate and highlight the values of The Wilderness Act on its 50th Anniversary in 2014.

Goal 3B: Advance and strengthen partnerships to facilitate shared stewardship and to advance the relevance of the NLCS to communities of interest and place.

1. Support attendance at Association of Public Lands Partners conferences and workshops by managers and non-governmental organizations.

2. Strengthen and support the cultural resource stewardship program – host the site stewardship training at NLCS units.

3. Work with the curation office to document, conserve and protect artifacts and historical objects for public use. Develop partnerships with local museums/historical societies to showcase recovered artifacts for public educational opportunities.

4. Support place-based partnerships such as Pompeys Pillar Historical Association, River and Plains Society, Friends of Missouri Breaks Monument, and the Missouri River Stewards.

5. Engage veterans through employment and mentoring programs such as Veterans Green Corps and Wounded Warriors.

Goal 3C: Expand use of volunteers within the NLCS.

1. Provide a full-time volunteer director in Montana/Dakotas or district offices dedicated to developing the volunteer program. This position would complete tasks such as:

   • Developing a volunteer action plan that identifies specific projects that are suitable for volunteers, organizing training opportunities, and conducting award ceremonies and other public recognition.

   • Training a cadre of volunteers to serve as volunteer coordinators in each region.

Montana Wilderness Association

The Montana Wilderness Association is a nonprofit 501(c)(3) organization helping to protect Montana's wilderness heritage, quiet beauty and outdoor traditions, now and for future generations. Each year, the MWA coordinates and leads wilderness hikes throughout the state to raise awareness and appreciation for natural areas. MWA members also participate in National Public Lands Day events and other stewardship projects throughout the year. In 2012, the MWA partnered with Rocky Mountain College to conduct a BioBlitz inventory of the Pryor Mountains Wilderness Study Area. Future projects include the development of a citizen monitoring program for wilderness and WSAs, as well as development of a geotourism product for southeastern Montana.

Holter Lake - Sleeping Giant Wilderness Study Area

- Providing outreach on volunteer opportunities via websites such as Volunteer.gov amd through partner organizations.

- Conducting outreach to statewide organizations such as Boy Scouts, Girl Scouts, 4-H, etc.

2. Develop volunteer travel opportunities with organizations such as American Hiking Society, to encourage stewardship and awareness of Montana's NLCS units.

Goal 3D: Engage the public in stewardship of the NLCS lands through education and interpretation.

1. Identify required skills sets for environmental education/interpretation and provide training to resource specialists.

2. Develop attractive educational kiosks to highlight the conservation system at high use sites, such as Pompey's Pillar, Fort Benton, Chain-of-lakes campgrounds, and the Madison River campsites/river access points.

3. Develop a Hands-on-the-Land site for the Western, Eastern, and Hi-Line districts.

- Develop K-12 youth programs to instill the values and benefits of the conservation lands.

- Integrate Project Archeology into HOL curriculum where relevant.

4. Integrate volunteer opportunities and ideas into annual planning (budget, project implementation, etc.)

5. Provide training and encourage development of Leave No Trace and Tread Lightly outreach capacity. Host a Leave No Trace Master's Course at an NLCS unit.

Goal 3E: Recruit, train, and mentor young people so that they may engage professionally in recreation, education, and stewardship on NLCS lands.

1. Build partnerships with institutions of higher education across Montana/Dakotas (private, public, tribal, etc.) by sponsoring internships and work-study programs such as the UMRBNM Indian Education Program, Pompeys Pillar National Monu-

ment/Montana State University-Billings student intern program, and the University of Montana Recreation Practicum program.

2. Use and expand agreements with tribal colleges to engage Native American youth and build tribal relationships in NLCS units.

3. Identify opportunities to host summer work experience students through local Human Resource Development Council offices. Assign a lead position to facilitate the development of work projects, logistics and training to accomplish work.

4. Develop an agreement and provide funding for statewide (or district) conservation corps crews with NLCS focus.

5. Ensure that youth work projects include an educational element and that youth are provided with mentorship and information about career pathways.

Pennsylvania Power and Light, LLC

Our biggest partnership in terms of financial contributions for the Lewis and Clark Trail is the BLM-Butte Field Office agreement with Pennsylvania Power and Light (PPL). Recreation enhancement measures were established through the Missouri/Madison Hydroelectric Re-licensing Project. PPL is committed under the license and the Missouri/Madison Comprehensive Recreation Management Plan MOU to provide annual and cost-share funding to BLM for recreation site maintenance, upgrades, construction, and where appropriate, land acquisitions. In addition, this utility company also assists with upgrading the Comprehensive Recreation Plan, visitor surveys, visitor use counting, condition assessments and interpretive/education projects.

The BLM-Butte FO is fortunate to have these guaranteed funds to plan on each year and has a strong working partnership with this utility company. These O&M funds can be used to offset direct labor, operational, maintenance and improvement costs at both fee and non-fee sites on the Missouri River (Holter and Hauser Reservoir Segment).

Upper Missouri River Breaks National Monument

Theme 4: Building upon BLM's Commitment to Conservation

Strategic Approach: Take advantage of opportunities to communicate the mission and value of NLCS to BLM staff and internal partners (RACs, formal cooperators).

Improve coordination of internal budget requests across all programs that contribute to management of NLCS units. Promote the concept of "seamless management" by emphasizing ecosystems, communities, and watersheds.

Goal 4A: Improve internal communication and understanding of the NLCS and its potential to enhance the BLM as a whole.

1. Create a Montana/Dakotas NLCS webpage that provides news and updates on issues and accomplishments, and provide website links to related educational and interpretive sites.

2. Develop a Montana/Dakotas NLCS communications toolkit (brochures, fact sheets, postcards, posters, videos) that highlights all Monument(s), Wild and Scenic Rivers, Wilderness/WSAs, and National Trails.

Goal 4B: Cultivate shared responsibility for the NLCS conservation mandate as an integral part of BLM's multiple-use, sustained-yield mission.

1. Establish a task force with staff and management representation to complete an implementation strategy and communicate NLCS guidance to the broader workforce.

2. Develop a policy and standardized process to provide internal notification for proposed or authorized rights-of-way and other use authorizations within NLCS units.

3. Establish a program to recruit and train conservation "change agents" - a cadre of enthusiastic communicators to conduct internal outreach.

4. Review and revise policies and best management practices to integrate conservation and NLCS concepts; for example, the Gold Book, land health standards, etc.

5. Extend detail opportunities to Emerging Leaders, Leadership Academy, and Presidential Management Fellows. Develop and maintain project lists for these employees to seek experience in the NLCS.

6. Maintain an up-to-date implementation strategy for national monuments and similar designations based on the approved RMP or the most recent management plan.

7. Develop a mentoring program to pass down critical conservation management skills while accomplishing priority workloads. Establish statewide teams to conduct inventories of wilderness characteristics, visual resources, and wild and scenic rivers.

Goal 4C: Clearly define, understand, and justify staffing needs, and administratively organize the NLCS areas to operate as a cross-cutting program within the BLM.

1. Coordinate with programs leads to ensure funding for interdisciplinary projects.

2. Develop integrated BPS proposals for landscape level projects and programs.

3. Develop staffing plans and associated funding requests.

Goal 4D: Ensure the National Conservation Lands budget is coordinated with the other BLM programs. Set clear expectations and procedures for interdisciplinary budget development, priority setting, and reporting of accomplishments.

1. Coordinate with other BLM programs to provide NLCS funding toward landscape level projects that involve lands both within and outside of conservation units.

2. Continue to prioritize funding for partnership development and capacity building to ensure the continuance of partnerships.

Student Conservation Association

The Student Conservation Association has been an active partner with the Upper Missouri River Breaks National Monument and Wild and Scenic River for the past decade. The SCA mission is "to build the next generation of conservation leaders and inspire lifelong stewardship of our environment and communities by engaging young people in hands-on service to the land." SCA works in partnership with BLM to provide direct service through its internship program. In past years, SCA interns have served in critical seasonal positions in river management and interpretive center programs. The interns provided outstanding support to the Interpretive Center by staffing the front desk, assisting the Interpretive Center Director with educational programs, and performing grounds keeping duties as required. On the river, interns staffed Visitor Contact Stations along the river corridor and assisted park rangers with visitor use collection data, campground maintenance, wilderness study area monitoring and river patrols. This agreement is instrumental in providing necessary on-site staffing and expertise, as well as fulfilling our commitment to employing youth in natural resources.

Humbug Spires Wilderness Study Area

BLM/MT/GI-13-006+610